MW01118667

The Golden Road:
Taking a Ride on the Road of Life with a
Traumatic Brain Injury

Written by Shawn Kelly

Edited by Mike McCullough
Cover Art by William Burke
Copyright (C) 2017

My first picture wearing a Wake Forest uniform (8/83)

The Golden Road: Taking a Ride on the Road of Life with a Traumatic Brain Injury is about me, but it's about much more than a single person. This story is about family, teamwork, friendship, and many people who have touched my life. This story is also about determination and the compassion of others.

I wrote this story in large part to show my appreciation to the many people who overwhelmed me with the compassion they have shared. It may just have been their nature to be compassionate, but it was my life!

The name of my book is <u>The Golden Road</u> for a couple of reasons. Wake Forest's colors are gold and black. But more importantly, I wanted to show how well I've traveled my Road. My Road might have had bumps, but it turned out being pretty smooth.

The Golden Road

I remember looking up and seeing a calendar on the wall. The date was August 5, 1985. The days before had been crossed out, leaving the 5th the next in order.

I remember lying in a hospital bed, trying to move, but couldn't. I was in a room by myself and I didn't know why. I remember yelling as loud as I could, but nobody came. It was like I was having a bad dream and nobody could hear me.

I wasn't scared. I was in a state of confusion. I'd be in one place and then another. I didn't know where the time went. You know how in dreams you just appear somewhere? That's the way it was for me! One thing would happen and then something totally different.

Somehow I knew I'd been in a car accident and I had been in the hospital for a long time. I didn't know how long, but it had been about four months.

My parents must have told me. They were the only people always in my dreams. They told me I had a breathing tube inserted. The trache – short for tracheotomy – had been removed, but it left lots of scar tissue in my throat.

That's why I couldn't talk, at least not very loud. To this day, I still have trouble with scar tissue making my voice sound crackled and raspy.

I remember being in a hospital room with my parents. A television was showing a video tape. The video tape was of a bunch of football players and coaches telling me to get better soon. A coach even yelled at me, demanding that I get to practice, saying they needed me for the upcoming season. I remember him saying with a colorful use of vocabulary that he was going to run me until I dropped.

That video tape reminded me that I played football for Wake Forest University. For the 1985 season, the team had my name printed on the left sleeve of their jerseys. I don't remember the date, but with my parents, I watched on television as they unveiled the jerseys. I remember the commentator saying that they were showing their support for a fallen teammate.

Wake Forest warming up. Notice the left sleeves of the jerseys - SHAWN.

Like a flood gate opening, watching the video tape washed over me with a lot of memories. I remembered practicing with those guys – not all of them, but some of them. I remembered dreaming about playing college football for years. Seeing that video tape inspired me – I couldn't let that dream die!

A football team is kind of like the military. You eat, sleep, and practice with the same group day in and day out. Your teammates kind of become your family. My "Brothers in Arms". I wanted to prove to them that I deserved their support.

I also felt it was a mandate for me to rejoin the team. That left me feeling energized! I started thinking that it would take me no time to get back in shape for football. Getting back in shape would be easy. I wanted to start rehabilitation now.

Little did I realize what lie waiting!

Where The Road Started

My dream of playing college football started when I was young. I began playing competitive football when I was eight years old. A teammate of mine from my little league days was Paul Palmer. He went on to be a star player at a rival high school that I played against a few years later.

In college at Temple University, Paul was a runner up for the Heisman Trophy in 1986. He played in the National Football League for Kansas City, Detroit, Cincinnati, Philadelphia, and Dallas. I remember seeing him score a touchdown on a kickoff return for the Cowboys. Years earlier in high school, when we were on opposing teams, he scored the same way.

Paul Palmer is running through a tackle.

The quarterback of my high school football team was Tony Dilweg. He was a year behind me.

After high school, Tony played college football at Duke University. Duke and Wake Forest are both members of the Atlantic Coast Conference (ACC). Tony graduated from Duke and went on to play football with Green Bay and Los Angeles.

Because of my auto accident, I never played against Tony in college which was good for him! While I was at Wake Forest and Tony was at Duke, Wake never lost a football game to Duke! Talk about bragging rights? I would've never let him live that down!

Tony wore the same number in Green Bay as Duke.

What Happened on The Road that Changed Everything

On May 14, 1985, I had a car accident near Charlottesville, Virginia. It was bad. Really bad.

I was driving home after spring semester final exams. I had a passenger with me, a teammate and 1982 ACC Rookie of the Year, Michael Ramseur. I was giving him a lift to his father's house in Washington, DC.

How the accident happened isn't clear to me. I don't remember the accident or most of the entire year before.

What I've been told is that another vehicle cut me off, causing my car to hit a guard rail on the right side of the highway, careen across three lanes of traffic and flip upside down. I ended up being thrown from the car, landing face-down in the median.

Luckily, Michael wasn't seriously injured. When the car started to flip, he got down on the floor boards. He's the one who possibly could've told the police that I was run off the road. Because no car ever stopped, the police weren't able to verify what exactly had happened.

I was driving a '57 Chevy 210 Hardtop. I loved that car. I would roll down the street with the engine roaring and radio blasting Billy Idol. That car turned a lot of heads. It changed something inside me: all of a sudden I was like a shooting star. I don't know what it was about that car: it just made me feel good! It was like a blast from the past!

From the scene of the accident, I was taken by helicopter to the hospital at the University of Virginia (UVA). I don't know whether I was given the trache breathing tube then or by first responders at the accident scene.

My parents told me that some of the interns were actually UVA football players who were training to become doctors. How do you like that? Fierce ACC football rivals of Wake Forest and now these guys are trying to save my life!

I was x-rayed from head to toe. The only broken bone was my thumb. But the x-rays also revealed my brain was swelling. I'd experienced a Traumatic Brain Injury. To deal with that, the physicians drilled holes in my skull to release the pressure.

When my parents arrived at the hospital, the doctors filled them in on my condition. I was in a deep coma. They didn't give me much of a chance. On the Glasgow Coma Scale, which is the medical standard for assessing levels of consciousness, I had very low response readings. The doctors even asked my folks if they could have my vital organs.

My father got angry and said "You do all you can do first, and then we will talk about it." He described the scene as a bunch of ghouls standing around wringing their hands together. He said it reminded him of a scene from an old horror flick. To him, it looked as if they were giving up!

My family being Catholic, my parents asked for the Last Rites to be administered.

There was something else the x-rays showed: the doctors found that my neck had been broken – but not in the car accident. Somehow my neck bone had healed itself. Calcium deposits had formed on my neck. The doctors were puzzled and questioned my father.

My dad remembered that when I was in high school, I complained about my neck hurting. My father has never played a down of football in his life. Do you know the advice he gave me? He told me "Just don't use it!"

You use your neck in nearly all aspects of football. A football player not using his neck is like a soccer player not using his feet. My father and I always got a big laugh out of that.

The UVA hospital is an amazing facility that's helped and still is helping countless patients. Even though they angered my father when they asked about donating my vital organs, they were only trying to save as many lives as possible. I will always be thankful for what they did for me immediately after my accident.

I found out later that among the first things they did at the hospital was insert tubes in the sides of my chest. They used the tubes to inflate my lungs because they had collapsed from hitting the ground when I was thrown out of my car.

Hitting the ground also caused my Traumatic Brain Injury. When they shaved my head in preparation to drill holes to reduce the pressure, the whole left side of my head was badly bruised.

The truth was my whole body was badly bruised. I looked like a billboard painted with different shades of black and blue. The surgeries left scars and those added streaks of red.

The reason for my scars could've been because UVA is a teaching hospital or it could have been the interns just wanted that leg up on next season by leaving their marks like Zorro!

When I was at UVA, my parents kind of pitched a tent in Charlottesville. My parents watched over me, same as they'd always done. They put me in a bed with side rails. The side rails went the entire length of the bed.

I've always been a real restless sleeper, moving a lot during the night. When I was younger, I fell out my bed at home many times. My parents said it would be no big deal to see me lying with my leg or arm over the side rail.

I was still feeling the effect of the coma. That was as far as I could straighten my arms and without the belt around my waist, I would have fallen out of the chair.

UVA was about 100 miles from my house. So my parents had me transferred to Suburban Hospital in Bethesda, Maryland. The hospital was right around the corner from my childhood home. It made it easier for my parents to maintain their continuous watch. I have no memory at all of being at that hospital.

When I arrived at Suburban, my father asked for a bed with side rails, explaining the reason why.

The doctors and nurses at Suburban said there was no need for a bed with side rails. My dad again explained the need for the side rails, but they were pretty emphatic.

That night the hospital called my parents, saying I fell out of bed. The staff was rushing me to get x-rays and reinstall my trache. Upon arriving at the hospital, my father was livid: "I told you this would happen. Why didn't you listen to me?"

It was the second time my parents had to deal with my trache. While I was at UVA right after my accident, my parents told me that they were asked to leave the room to allow the nurses to wash me or something like that.

When they returned, I was blue and in distress. My parent called the nurses in a panic. According to my father, one of the nurses said, "Oops, it looks like we reinstalled the trache wrong." I'm sure they didn't really say 'oops' – my father might of been stretching the truth a little bit.

Anyway, the x-rays they took came back negative. It goes without saying they found a bed with side rails.

I did start to make a noticeable recovery. I was in the final stages of the coma. The doctors removed the trache. My eyes were opening and I began to recognize people and things. I even started to say a few words.

It must have been hard for my family. Besides wondering if I would recognize them, they also wondered if they would be able to understand me. The first words out of my mouth were in French. I had just finished my second semester of French.

Even with the language barrier, the staff was focused on teaching me how to walk. That process started with strengthening muscles that had atrophied while I was in the coma.

They had me exercising on a tilt table. They had me rocking forward and backward on a mat. They had me trying to walk between two parallel bars. They were willing to do anything to help regain the ability to walk.

Suburban specializes in stroke treatment. Strokes are very closely associated with Traumatic Brain Injuries. Strokes are caused by blood clots traveling through the blood stream to the brain while Traumatic Brain Injuries are caused by external impact to the brain.

Both involve an injury to brain, but most patients with Traumatic Brain Injuries are usually younger and require a different set of therapies.

So my parents had me transferred to Mt. Vernon Hospital. The hospital was in Virginia, about 45 minutes from our house. And Mt. Vernon specializes in treating Traumatic Brain Injuries like mine.

At Mt. Vernon, they actually tied me down in bed. They weren't going to let me fall out of bed!

The Road to Recovery

Soon after I arrived at Mt. Vernon, my day-to-day memory started to improve. Maybe it was because of therapies I was receiving or maybe it was simply time.

I think it was the latter, because I couldn't really start the Speech or Cognitive therapies until I could remember from day to day. It could've been the therapies or therapists that jarred my memory. They would like to think so, I guess.

Something a little funny happened in therapy one day. Remember when I said that the only broken bone I suffered in the accident was my thumb? Well, I was with my therapist and my thumb started bleeding. It didn't hurt – it just started bleeding!

I was a little puzzled, so I said, "Look at this!" The therapist replied, "Your pin is coming out." Pin? What pin? She told me that my thumb had been broken and the doctors used a pin to fuse my thumb bone together. That was the first time

I heard about the pin or that my thumb had been broken – talk about playing dumb!

At the time, I felt like a tree with my roots stuck in the ground. I was stiff as a board. At UVA, they said that I curled up into the fetal position. The contracting of arms and legs is a stage measured on the Glasgow Coma Scale.

When I got to Mt. Vernon, I was still tighter than a ball of yarn. I'm still stiff after more than 30 years, in some ways, it's like the accident happened yesterday.

I still have a mark on my arm from where a therapist tried pulling my arm straight. The scar is on my right arm at the elbow. The therapist stopped stretching my arm. It hurt and I yelled. Well, I still couldn't yell very loud.

I asked the therapist not to stop. She said you are yelling and it's hurting you. I said "So what? If you don't stretch it, my arm will never straighten out." From that point on, I knew that whenever she was stretching my arm, I couldn't make a sound.

Even though I stopped yelling, I think she stopped trying as hard. My arms are still not right. My left arm is not so noticeable, but my right is noticeably bent.

It seemed like a no-brainer to start working out. They called it Physical Therapy. Physical Therapy is a great thing. Any other athlete and I would call it conditioning. Well, they are very closely related. The real difference is Physical Therapy usually involves just one muscle. Conditioning involves the whole body.

I always questioned the therapists: Why couldn't I do more? Why couldn't I do this? Why couldn't I do that? I had spent at least half of my life conditioning or rehabilitating myself.

I was used to working hard for football, always trying to condition myself. They would tell me not to, but I would walk around when the nurses weren't looking. I walked in closed areas of the hospital so no one would notice.

I remember my mother arguing with my father one time. My parents would take me to a secluded part of the hospital that was being remodeled. With my father's help, I would walk around. My mother was always scared we would get caught. The hospital was so afraid of lawsuits; they wouldn't let me or anyone else work on their own. At least, that is my take.

When I couldn't get the results I wanted from Physical Therapy, I started pushing in Speech and Cognitive therapies. I wanted more and faster. I think that those two therapies were the most important parts to my recovery. I was used to rehabilitating myself physically, but not mentally.

I expressed my displeasure with the hospital staff to my parents over and over again. It was all I would talk about. My parents knew me and the drive I possessed. They believed in me. They knew that I wouldn't stop until I got to where I wanted to be.

Bill Faircloth, a coach from Wake Forest, once said that being so driven – or stubborn – could sometimes get me in trouble. This time it worked, because my father told the staff that he was going to pull me out of the hospital if they didn't release me. Since the hospital didn't want that on their record, they went ahead and released me. But I would continue to go to daily therapy.

After nearly six months in the hospital, I remember the day I was released. My whole family and I went down to Winston-Salem to see a Wake Forest football game against Maryland.

I'm talking with Coach Faircloth before the Maryland game. Look at how stiff I looked, even though the accident was six months earlier.

I remember bursting into a team meeting upon arrival. I was on Cloud 9 when everyone started cheering for me. I can't exactly describe the feeling I had except that it was overpowering.

After the game, Maryland's coach Bobby Ross came to the Wake Forest sideline to shake my hand. Maryland had recruited me in high school, so I guess they got word of my accident somehow. While I was in the hospital, Bobby had mailed letters to my parents expressing his hope for my full recovery.

Bobby Ross was the head coach for the San Diego Chargers.

My excitement continued the next day. After the game, a television crew interviewed Wake's Head Coach Al Groh and me. I really didn't know how to answer the questions asked, but Coach Groh and the reporter filled in all the empty spots.

Some of my teammates reminded me of a story about Coach Groh that happened during the previous season. We were getting ready to play North Carolina and he was trying to inspire us. He was telling us about an Alaskan fisherman.

It was during the winter and the fisherman would do anything to feed his family. In order to keep the worm warm before putting it on the hook, he'd put the worm in his mouth. In the locker room before the kick off, Coach Groh pulled out this worm put in his mouth. Asking us the question, "What are you going to do to win?" The locker room exploded! We won the game 14-3.

Head Coach, Al Groh at the University of Virginia which was his alma mater.

The North Carolina game was also the first televised football game that I'd played. It was the first opportunity for my family and friends from Maryland (Wake was a 7 or 8 hour drive from Bethesda) to see me compete at the college level.

I was on the kickoff team. I ran out on the field and got in position. The excitement was pumping through my body. Then the referee signaled for a commercial timeout!

Anyway, on the drive back to Bethesda after the Maryland game, we stopped by UVA hospital, where my Golden Road started. My parents exchanged greetings with the doctors and nurses, who then went on with their daily activities. Some were talking with each other, making faces and pointing at me.

The attention made me feel very uncomfortable. I was already self-conscious about the way I looked and moved. The last thing I wanted to do was draw attention to myself.

When it came time to leave, I was the first out the door. As soon as the door opened, I drew a straight line for the car.

As we left the parking lot, the rest of my family wanted to eat at local restaurant. I said "No, let's go. I just want to get out of here."

My father must have realized that I felt uncomfortable. He explained that the reason everyone was staring was because they couldn't believe I was the same person they had treated earlier and the progress I'd made.

Family Involvement on My Road

While I was in the hospital, my family was always there. As I said before, they watched over me. My pain was their pain. I know it's easy to think that you're the only one going through it, but you're not!

My mother saw me reaching for the phone next to my hospital bed. Not only did she wonder what I was doing, but she was kind of excited to see me actually trying to do something.

I know that sounds kind of funny, but after weeks of just lying in bed without any movement, any activity was a refreshing change.

She asked, "Who do you want to call?" With what must of sounded like a whisper, I said, "My mother." Can you imagine how she felt? I didn't recognize my own mother, but she was the first person that I wanted to call.

Don't be naive and think that you're the only one hurting!

The Road Back to School

Before the Christmas of '85, I called Coach Groh. I asked would it be possible to return to Wake Forest. He was excited that I wanted to return and agreed to my return.

It didn't go very well with my therapists when I told them of my plan go back to Wake Forest. One even told me that "You couldn't even sit in a class for fifty minutes much less pass the course. The only job you'll ever qualify for will be manual labor."

I didn't yell. I just stood up and walked out, never to return. I remember heading to the car yelling and throwing punches in the air because I was so mad. Not that I had something against manual labor jobs: a good honest day's work is good for the mind and body. But I knew the pay wouldn't get me the things I wanted out of life. I was trying to move forward and they were holding me back.

The next morning my mother tried to get me to go to therapy, but I wouldn't go! I remember saying that I'd never go back. My mother is pretty strong minded, but I wouldn't budge. I never gave up on anything easily and I wasn't going to start now.

Soon after New Year's Day, Coach Groh called my parents. He reiterated how excited he was that I wanted to come back to Wake. After thinking about it, he thought Wake Forest might be too difficult.

My parents discussed it with me and I agreed to take a couple of classes at a local community college. It was not what I wanted, but if taking some courses at the local community college could help get me back to Wake, I'd do it.

The community college was about 30 minutes away and my parents didn't feel safe with me driving. So my father signed up for night classes with times that corresponded to mine.

He used that time to evaluate my driving skills. I remember we drove a 4-speed Chevy S-10. The S-10 had a small V-6 engine, so it didn't have much power. The S-10 also needed a new battery, because the battery never held a charge. Whenever I would stall it, we needed to jump it. So it was kind of out of necessity that I learned to drive a stick well.

This is the '57 210 Hardtop. I restored after the accident. The S-10 truck is in the background.

I was also rehabilitating myself physically. All of those years of football conditioning started paying off in ways I never planned. It was like the start of a new season. I was conditioning my mind as well as my body. I ran a quarter mile and slowly I built up to a mile.

On the mental side, my parents asked an old high school football coach (who was also a Special Ed teacher) to tutor me. I was getting ready for football and school. Or so I thought. I even took the savings I had and bought another '57 Chevy (and painted it maroon).

After completing the courses at the community college (I received a 'B' and a 'C'), I called Coach Groh back and asked if I could return. He said that I'd earned it and agreed to my return for a summer school session. I was overjoyed. I was on my way.

I continued rehabilitating myself physically. My father got me an old Chevy Impala. The car was a faded gray and my brother spray painted 'Gray Ghost' on the trunk as a joke. After making sure it was road worthy, my parents sent me off to Wake.

Reality set in after the first couple of days of summer school. I didn't even remember a single professor or a class that I had taken at Wake much less the content.

I also realized that the couple months of training didn't compare to the years of running and weight lifting that I used to get the scholarship in the first place. When the accident occurred my weight was 260 pounds. While I was in the hospital, I lost 90 pounds.

I had gained some weight back, but I was still a shell of my former self. I was humbled by the speed and strength of my teammates. It was hard even for me to believe that I once competed at that level.

I also realized the community college didn't prepare me for the educational challenges and demands I'd face at Wake Forest. The classes were tough. I had to read a chapter over and over just to achieve the knowledge or understanding to follow along in class. I never seemed to catch up. It always seemed to be a day or two later that I would begin to understand.

It also didn't help that the letters on the page were all blurry. I needed glasses: I didn't need them before. I later found out that loss of sight is another side effect of having a Traumatic Brain Injury.

My hearing was a problem too. They told me that hearing loss is another result of a Traumatic Brain Injury. But I wonder if it might not have been from blasting my radio in the '57 Chevy. I refused to use the hearing aids back then, but now I can't function without them.

When I first checked into the athletic dorms for summer school, I was introduced to an in-coming freshman named Ricky Proehl. I later saw him play in three Super Bowls with St. Louis, Carolina, and Indianapolis. He played for seven different teams over a seventeen year career. He played in four Super Bowls, winning two. The last I heard, he retired as the wide receiver coach for the Carolina Panthers.

Ricky Proehl playing with the Chicago Bears

I also learned that my jersey number was being used by someone else. I was angry! I still had dreams of playing.

As an athlete, your number is special to you. Everybody identifies you with that number. There is something that is almost superstitious or mythical about your jersey number and only the player wearing it knows how to describe that feeling.

They gave my number to an offensive lineman. His name was Tony Mayberry. After college, Tony went on to play center for Tampa Bay and was named to the Pro Bowl three times. Thinking back now, I guess it was alright for him to wear my number!

All-Pro Tony Mayberry

One of my first memories of Wake Forest is about basketball, not football. I was coming in the door of the athletic dorms with one of my teammates. After finishing practice, eating dinner, and walking back to the dorms on a hot evening in North Carolina, I was tired.

Coming in, I saw three or four basketball players. I knew they were basketball players because they were all very tall except for one. This little guy was yelling at the bigger basketball players. I turned and asked my teammate, "Who's that little guy talking all of that trash?"

My teammate told me that he was a new kid from Baltimore named Muggsy Bogues. Muggsy was only 5'3". That's pretty short for a basketball player. Or so I thought that day.

I told my teammate Muggsy better be able to play, because as much stuff as he's talking, he's going to get hurt. I had no way of knowing then that Muggsy would be selected in the first round of the NBA draft and have an outstanding professional career – including, believe it or not, winning the slam dunk competition at one year's All Star Game! He was the shortest player ever to play in the NBA.

I think that if Muggsy knew what I said that day, he'd probably ask me, "How do you like me now?"

I wonder what Michael is telling Muggsy

I didn't do well that summer session. I was only taking one class, but I still couldn't handle it. To make matters worse, I was already on academic probation because before my accident I didn't really take school seriously. My GPA reflected that.

I remember going home and waiting by the phone and hoping they would give me another chance. Coach Faircloth called to tell me they did give me that chance.

I came to the realization that my football days were over. That was a very hard thing for me to accept, but I knew I could never get back in good enough shape to play at the college level. The accident left me with permanent right arm and leg damage. There was nothing I could do that would change that reality.

I had dreamed of playing college football for years. I remembered lettering and traveling with the team. I remembered flying to the different cities and staying in hotels the night before games. I played with and against a lot of players who went on to play professionally. I remembered young kids asking for my autograph. But I was only a role player, never a starter. I only got a glimpse of the good life.

I didn't give up on my education. I was going to get that degree that my therapist thought was unattainable. My days were left free to study, but I was distracted very easily and couldn't concentrate for any length of time. For that reason and to save on costs, my parents asked me to become a part-time student.

I would use the athletic facilitates a lot. Whether it was to run, lift weights, or just talk to a coach or one of my teammates. I even joined a fraternity – Kappa Sigma. But I knew everything took second place to school.

The administration and professors at Wake Forest were great. They worked hard with me in order to obtain my goal. The administration allowed me to change my major, transfer credits from the community college, and allowed me to be one of the first students to register for class each semester. The professors allowed me to take extra-long completing the exams and would reiterate directions or assignments. The professors sometimes would even give me one-on-one tutoring.

It's my hope that my entire Wake Forest family – the administration, the professors, the students, my coaches, and my teammates – really understand all they've done for me and how much appreciation I have for them.

That was especially true my first couple of semesters back. It seemed as if every week I would go and see someone in the administration office. Also, I was continually asking for a tutor's or a professor's assistance.

I remember one time driving to a professor's office to get help. The professor was a part-time professor who worked full time at the Wake Forest's affiliated hospital, Wake Forest Baptist

Medical Center. She tutored me for an hour every day for about week. I was able to freely ask questions that I wouldn't have asked in class because I didn't have to worry about slowing things down for the other students.

My fellow students and teammates were always helping me, whether it be tutoring me or just providing an example of what a student/athlete should be.

Before the accident, I discovered up close and personal why a hill next to the gym was called Termite Hill. I skipped class one morning during Spring Football. It was an eight a.m. class and I didn't feel like getting up.

My position coach found out and, after practice that day, I ran that hill until I dropped and was crawling up it like a termite. It was the same coach who appeared in the team video yelling at me and telling me he was going to run me until I dropped. I tried very hard never to miss a class again. If I did, I had a very good reason!

I took an American Literature course to fulfill one of my requirements to graduate. I remember reading a story by Mark Twain. The story was called the "Jumping Frog of Calaveras County."

I read other pieces of literature earlier for the course. Sometimes I would get the point and sometimes I wouldn't. My professor told me to read deeper. I said "You mean like an underlying meaning?" She said, "Not really an underlying meaning. You just need to read deeper."

I read that story over and over again. Finally, I realized that the stranger had fed the frog lead shot ammo. If you have never read the story, a stranger feeds Jim Smiley's frog shot while Jim had his back turned. By the time Jim realizes what happened, the stranger was nowhere to be found. I learned to read figuratively, not just literally.

Hoping to be able to help people who had been in an accident like mine, I majored in Psychology. Being a doctor was out of the question, seeing that life sciences were not my good suit.

Psychology is a behavioral science and Psychology seemed to come natural to me.

Majoring in Psychology, I learned about the Cross Brain Theory. The Cross Brain Theory states that when you sustain damage to one side of your brain, it affects the muscles of the opposite side of your body. In my case, my head had sustained damage on the left side. So my right leg and arm were affected.

I also learned that you don't really lose memories. You really only lose the memory pointers to those passageways in the brain. When the brain has a traumatic event, it loses the pointers. It's the way the brain defends itself.

It's funny. I mentioned earlier that I remember looking up and seeing that calendar on the wall in my hospital room at Mt. Vernon. But I don't remember much of the year before. It's like time stopped and started again. Some memories came back easily, but there are things I'll never remember.

I do remember dessert in the dining hall at Wake Forest. It was the Friday following spring football practice. My roommates and I decided to play some softball. We also decided to chip in for a keg of beer. It goes without saying that by dinner time, we all had had a little too much to drink – well, I was fine, it was my teammates who had had a little too much!

I was getting my dinner selection on the training line and then deciding on dessert. I grabbed two pieces of strawberry shortcake. Ms. Juanita, who was my favorite cafeteria employee and knew I had a sweet tooth, said, "You're going to get sick eating all that dessert." I proceeded to eat about twenty shortcakes just out of spite. She and I always got a laugh out that.

Oh, by the way, I didn't get sick!

After three years and all the summer school I could get, I graduated with a degree in Psychology. It took me two years before the accident and three years after.

Wake Forest is one of the most respected colleges in the nation and my Golden Road went through Wake Forest. It took me longer and it wasn't easy, but I graduated! And because Wake Forest is also very strong in the Liberal Arts, I was able to take a lot of courses outside of my major.

The Road Goes On

I remember watching television when the Buffalo Bills were playing Super Bowl XXV. All-Pro, Bruce Smith came out of the game due to an equipment problem. I remember seeing his replacement trot out on the field and thinking to myself that he looked like Gary Baldinger.

Here is Gary Baldinger practicing with the Buffalo Bills.

Gary was the starter ahead of me at Wake Forest. I had to watch a lot of practice film and Gary moved distinctively, so I knew that about him. As he got in position the announcer call out his name. I knew I was right – it was Gary! I saw him recently at Wake Forest and he told me that he played in the NFL for Buffalo, Indianapolis, Kansas City, and Tennessee.

I also recognized the way another former teammate moved. I was watching ESPN and they were showing highlights of the World Football League championship. I saw one of the quarterbacks dropping back for a pass and swore to myself that he looked like Mike Elkins. Then the announcer said the quarterback was Mike Elkins! Mike was the starting quarterback at Wake Forest. He was drafted in the early second round of the 1989 draft by Kansas City. He also played with Cleveland, Houston, and the World Football League's Sacramento Surge.

Here is Mike Elkins playing for the Sacramento Surge.

Further Down The Road

Seeing my former teammates playing at the professional level was great, but I was at a crossroad. It has been months and I still didn't have a job. I naively thought employers would be knocking down my door!

My father helped me land a spot with the federal government that didn't really have much to do with my degree in Psychology. It was in Cartography – which is a big word for 'making maps.'

With my degree from Wake Forest, I only needed ten more credit hours in earth science, math, or computer science to qualify as a Cartographer. So, I went back to the same community college as before to complete some additional classes. Because of the education that I received at Wake Forest, I completed those additional classes easily.

Even though I completed the additional classes, I didn't officially start my new job until nine months later. I was fortunate to be able to live with my parents. I took on whatever employment I could find, mostly doing odd jobs. I cut grass, pumped gas, and worked on a construction crew. I was becoming more and more discouraged as the months passed. I was elated when the government finally gave me a starting date.

My first day at my new job, they told us we were all going to become Computer Specialists. I first graduated with a degree in Psychology, went back to school in order to become a Cartographer, and now I was being told I was going to become a Computer Specialist. I credit Wake Forest for giving me the background to allow me to do it.

With all the changes going on in my life, I had a very steep learning curve in my new job. I was also at the wrong end of the curve. I was going to be using a database and a user interface.

I'd heard of databases and user interfaces before, but I didn't have much experience with them. I couldn't even type. In fact, up until that moment, I had never really used a computer for anything other than playing games and some word processing. So I attended classes to learn about different computer components. The classes were six hours daily and 3-5 days long depending on the class. I struggled. It was hard for me to stay focused for six hours, especially when I questioned everything!

The government agency I worked for at the time was in the beginning stages of developing the architecture for a new program. That was a good thing, because I grew with the architecture and it wasn't so obvious that I was struggling. In fact, by the time the program was fully developed, I had kind of specialized on one component and I became one of the in-house experts for a mainframe database known as Model 204.

About a year and a half after I started my job, I met my future wife, Jackie. Three months after meeting her, I proposed. A little over three months later, we got married. The ceremony was held in the same church where Jackie's parents got married and on the same day as my parents' 29th anniversary. Now I had a partner traveling with me on my Golden Road.

I wanted our wedding to be a very intimate with a large reception. At the wedding itself, we only had immediate family. Later at the reception, we had close to two hundred friends and relatives.

Jackie and I deciding who's going to get the first piece in '92.

Before the wedding, we were trying to decide on a honeymoon. That year Wake Forest was playing in the Independence Bowl in Shreveport, Louisiana. So I convinced Jackie to spend our honeymoon around a bunch of football players and coaches.

She said later the one good thing about going to the Independence Bowl was she felt very small. I'm hoping that was not the only good thing about our honeymoon for her! Oh, Wake won! We beat Oregon by a score of 39–35.

The Road had Bends

At first, I was very happy working for the government, but later I let my ego get the best of me. I thought I was not being paid what I deserved. I saw my classmates and friends making big salaries and I wanted to join them.

One reason why I may have wanted big money was our expanding family. Our Road was blessed with three kids -- Patrice, Christian and Shannon. But I realized that another reason was my competitiveness. I believed I could compete in the private sector. Sure my family had gotten bigger and I wanted to get them the best, but it was my ego!

I took a job with the UNISYS Corporation, a government contractor, with a salary more in line with the private sector. I did really well for a while programming in Model 204, but I let my illusions get the best of me again.

At the time, Oracle Corporation, based in Redwood, California was exploding on the market. Oracle, to this day, is an international leader in developing database software. What really made them successful early on was that their software was 'portable' while mainframe databases (like Model 204) weren't. The market was changing and the demand was for 'portability.'

All five of us at Patrice's first communion (4/01).

I struggled through the training, but got a certification and landed a new job using Oracle within UNISYS. I lived to regret my decision.

With the government, I was allowed to grow with the architecture. Working as a contractor, you are expected to hit the ground running. That just wasn't me.

UNISYS laid me off. I was upset, but wasn't angry with them. If it were me, I would have done the same thing. I took a detour on my journey or maybe a wrong turn.

Maybe the therapists were right. Maybe all I could do was manual labor. I even began to doubt myself. But I couldn't believe that! There was no way that I could have any doubts! I had a family now. I had others people relying on me.

I wanted to go back to working for the government. A government job meant security for me. In the government, I would have a better chance at being successful. I swallowed my pride and again cut grass in order to make ends meet. I used the off hours to apply for government jobs. I even took a job as a hospital transporter, pushing around patients in wheelchairs at Suburban Hospital – the same place where I was earlier on my journey. The whole time I thought I was just spinning my wheels.

I recall having twenty government interviews. I interviewed all over the place inside the DC beltway. I decided to expand my search to all government agencies, no matter the location. I even applied for jobs at a lower grade or pay level.

After ten months of applying, I finally landed back in the government. My new job was located in Gloucester, Massachusetts. Now, our Golden Road went through the oldest seaport in America.

I landed a job at the National Marine Fishery Service. It was difficult for my family to move away from the only place they ever knew. But I think they adjusted well and I feel we have grown as a family.

The position was as a junior Oracle Forms developer. I had seen Oracle Forms before and even used Forms, but I knew it was going to be a slow process to become a journeymen developer. However, I was back in the government, where I thought I would be given the time I needed to become a good programmer.

I arrived on Massachusetts' scenic Cape Ann a couple of days early to get myself situated. I found a vacation rental apartment that I leased for three months while I explored the town of Gloucester and nearby towns of Rockport, Manchester-by-the-Sea, and Essex.

Because I'd started my job during the school year, it was our decision to let the kids finish the year in Maryland. I had found a house and bought it, but for a while without my family it felt pretty empty.

My first day on the job everybody seemed so nice. From my earlier exploration trips, I found the surroundings -- the beaches and lighthouses -- to be very beautiful and picturesque. I thought I had made a good move in coming to this fishing town.

My initial sense of calm after relocating ended soon enough when I learned the Fisheries used a sink-or-swim approach. In other words, they gave you a manual, sent you to a few classes, and expected you to start programming. It was hard to get any help because everyone was so busy.

I sank! I was taking longer to learn in my new position than the other programmers. I tried, but I couldn't learn fast enough. Because of this, I was given a new position every few years. They took me out of software programming and pushed me into hardware where I had very little experience.

I started working at the agency's Help Desk, performing computer security updates for most of the computers within the agency – it was called 'Patch Management'. That position included performing vulnerability checks and outputting reports for all the machines having access to the agency's network. The position required me to know a lot about a wide range of computer operating systems. I struggled. The agency then bought a new software package that allowed most of the updates to be performed at night by the agency's server. Again my position changed.

My new position involved completing a setup of the ever-changing software packages on the agency's multimedia computers. The multimedia computers were used for showing all presentations by personnel at the Fisheries. Each time a multimedia event took place, requested software packages had to be installed on the multimedia computers. And when the computers were shut down, all of the newly installed software was erased. So I had to reinstall the software packages each time anyone used a multimedia computer.

To compound my situation, the software packages kept changing and I had to keep learning about a huge range of computer types, makes, and models. I struggled! A lot!

Navigating Bends in The Road

At the time, my father owned an apartment complex in Bethesda. We originally moved in to the complex when I was four and my father later purchased it when I was eight. After my father's purchase, our family performed the role of residential manager. Because I was looking to provide college educations for my three kids and to create an emergency fund, I purchased rental properties.

Owning rental property was something I was comfortable with doing, I thought. I wanted to feel good in my job at the Fisheries, but couldn't. I hoped to fill the void by becoming a property owner. Beside the tenants shuffling in and out, the basic maintenance of an apartment building was routine for me. It seemed to be a good idea!

I had my ups and downs with my first rental property, but I convinced myself that owning more properties was the only way to go. I already owned a three-unit property and, after a few years, I purchased a six-unit and then a nine-unit property.

I don't know why I convinced myself owning more would be better, but I quickly became overwhelmed. My new properties became more work than I anticipated. Five months after buying my last property I decided to get out of the real estate business. Plain and simple, it involved too much of my time.

After a few months, I accepted an offer for all three properties. The selling process dragged on and on. What should have taken a month or two ended up taking four.

What was worse was the management at my full time job with the Fisheries took notice. It wasn't long afterward that my manager fired me, saying it was due to misuse of government equipment.

What I think is they were just looking for an excuse to get rid of me and I gave them what they needed. After twenty five years working for government or as a government contractor, they fired me. That emergency fund I had created really made sense now!

I was first and foremost fearful for my family. I just lost one of my life lines! I spent the following days locked in the house. I was embarrassed, humiliated, and ashamed.

I had lost the ability to provide for my family in the fashion we had grown accustomed to. I didn't know what to do. The only chance I had was to appeal my removal. The lawyers that I hired told me it was going to be a long battle.

I spent the days at home hiding myself from the world. I would hope nobody would come to the door. I screened all calls and would only accept ones from my wife and kids. I didn't want even to talk to my mother or my in-laws.

I felt like a big fat failure. I told my immediate family and my closest friends, and asked them not tell anyone else. My next door neighbors, who I had grown very close to, told their adult kids when they asked about me, that I had already retired and now was trying to get a pension. They added that I was having a hard time with it. It made me feel a little better that they felt compassion for me.

My family normally went back to Maryland for the holidays, but not this time. I wanted to conserve our money for necessities like food, taxes, and electricity. My wife took on more hours at her work and my kids didn't complain.

They knew what was going on, but took it all in stride. I could tell my wife was worried, but she tried not to show it. It was the second time we went through this, only now I was older and I had no prospects. I had really dug my family into a hole this time.

I would find myself awakening at night in a panic. I would be sweating and my heart would be racing. It was an awful feeling. I felt helpless! I'm supposed to be the provider – the head of the family.

I was thinking what would my family do? What would we eat? Where would we live? It would take me fifteen to thirty seconds to realize where I was and that I was only dreaming.

I decided that instead of appealing my removal, I would ask for disability retirement. The lawyers I hired to appeal the case asked me to have a neuropsychologist perform an evaluation.

I didn't want to be evaluated, because I didn't want to be reminded of what I already knew – that I'd suffered a Traumatic Brain Injury.

That was a fact I was continuously trying to conceal. I think it is easy to understand why I wanted to hide that fact. On the one hand, if I hadn't hidden that fact, I wouldn't be where I'm today. No one would have given me a chance if they knew everything about me.

Actually, I wouldn't really describe what I did as hiding the truth. I wasn't hiding anything. I just didn't want to make it too obvious. My physical handicaps were obvious. I just didn't want to show my mental handicaps.

The neuropsychologist said I had a cognitive impairment across multiple cognitive domains including learning, memory, language processing, executive functioning, and fine motor speed and dexterity.

She also said I meet the criteria for a Major Neuro-Cognitive Disorder. She said I found it very difficult to communicate and express my thoughts. She also determined that I had a slowly progressive cognitive decline (a pattern consistent with many individuals who have sustained a Traumatic Brain Injury).

I called the Social Security Administration to put in a claim for disability insurance. When I got through to them, they asked why I was claiming a disability. I told them that I suffered a bad car accident and suffered a Traumatic Brain Injury in 1985.

Jackie and I (9/16).

They said they just don't give disability to just anyone who claims to have had a Traumatic Brain Injury. I had to prove it! I would need a doctor to document my condition with test results.

I said no problem: I had just had a neuropsychological evaluation performed. They also told me if I could produce the documentation, I'd be given disability insurance.

They explained that having a Traumatic Brain Injury is a debilitating condition no matter when it happens. They went on to say that most people who have had a Traumatic Brain Injury make a claim right way. I never even thought about it until now. It's really something I should've known, but if I had claimed disability earlier, I wouldn't have had all experiences I've had or done the things I've done.

I was beginning to feel better about my situation. I was going to get Social Security disability, so I knew I wasn't going to be completely without retirement income. But I wanted to retire from the Fisheries. I wanted them to understand I wasn't trying to cheat them. My issues were real.

My primary physician called for a CAT scan of my brain, because he wanted some up-to-date imagery of my brain. After the CAT scan, the technician who administered the test confirmed what I had always known.

I didn't look at the images when he shook his head and said, "Oh, I see the old injury, but don't see anything new." I don't know, but I think he was a little surprised that I was doing as well as I was doing.

After hearing that I had suffered a Traumatic Brain Injury, the judge presiding over my case said that I should be retired. My lawyers said they drilled pretty hard on that point. The government conceded and asked that they be provided some doctor's proof.

My lawyers said they already had the documentation and the government lawyers would have it the next day. That day I knew I had won the case. My lawyers had proven to them that I was really disabled. We settled the case and I'm officially retired.

Where The Road Took Me

I had been employed in the federal government or by a government contractor for about twenty five years. I worked as a Model 204 Database Administrator, Oracle Database Administrator, Oracle Forms Developer, Security Analyst/Patch Management Technician and a Help Desk Analyst.

Things are getting progressively harder for me. Every morning, I have to stretch to just get moving. I have made stretching a part of my morning ritual. I still feel like that tree, but now my roots have gotten even longer. I hate to admit it, but my memory is becoming an issue. People are always repeating stuff that I should've remembered. Most times, I can blame it on my hearing. "Oh, I didn't hear you say that!"

Sometimes, life gets very frustrating. People are always asking if I came from the south. They say I talk slow and with a southern accent. I tell them it's because I went to college in North Carolina.

The real reasons why I speak like I do is the accident and resulting trache. People laugh at the way I walk. I walk with a limp, especially when I'm tired. Bartenders are always denying me alcohol. They say I've already had enough, when I haven't even had one.

In fact, remember me mentioning the '57 Chevy I bought after the accident? After I graduated from Wake and got a job, with my brother's help I restored that car. I took a number of years, but I restored it!

The '57, Jackie and I used in our wedding.

I proudly used it at my wedding with Jackie. Leaving our reception, the police stopped us for not having brake lights. My brother and I tried to repair the heating system earlier that day and inadvertently blew the fuse controlling the brake lights.

Anyway, the police asked me to get out of the car. When they saw me walk, they immediately gave me a breathalyzer test. That night the only drink I had was when the best man toasted our marriage. I remember the cops telling me, "We won't arrest you – it's your wedding night."

Arrest me for what? After the breathalyzer test came back negative, the officers left without another word. I will always think they were so embarrassed by having jumped to an unfair conclusion. I'll bet they would have arrested me on the spot if I had blown positive!

My brother, Chris was my best man in my wedding

Sometimes people ask me if I'm angry about the accident. They say they would be fighting mad, especially because the car that probably caused the accident never stopped.

I look at the past, learn from it, and move on. I learned from football that when you lose a game, you learn from your mistakes, and move on to the next game. In my case, I really just wanted to move forward. I was persistent and persevered. I'm trying to teach my kids that.

In some ways, I think I'm lucky that the accident happened when it did. First, I was young and my body was very resilient. I know I wouldn't have made such a good recovery if I hadn't been young.

Second, the accident happened while I was in college at Wake Forest. I was in a learning environment and surrounded by youth. I also had the advantage of being able to use the athletic facilities for my rehabilitation.

I had access to tutors whenever I needed the help. And I needed a lot of help. And it was there. In a way, I had everything going for me.

I feel like it's time for me to do something new. I know I will have to start at the bottom and work my way up again with whatever I do. I have to find something that fits my physical and mental limitations. Right now, I feel as though I'm letting those people down who helped optimize my chances for a good life.

When I look back on that period in my life surrounding the accident, I realize that I'm now kind of grateful for things the way they are. Sure, you always imagine how things could've been. But I look at all of the things I have now.

I have a wonderful wife, three terrific kids, a college education, and our house. I spent twenty five years employed and I'm now retired. If things had happened differently, I wouldn't have all these things.

If I would have listened to my therapists in our last meeting, I wouldn't be where I am today. You can't put limits on yourself. It isn't easy and there are always going to be hurdles, but you have to keep pushing through every roadblock.

What I've Learned From The Golden Road

My journey – The Golden Road – is about teamwork. It's about my family, friends and so much more. My parents gave me everything I needed to start in the right direction. My friends, teammates, coaches, and teachers kept steering me back on course. My wife and family were always there to show compassion, especially when the road got winding.

My journey is about using all resources available. I had great doctors and therapists to care for and help me. I had wonderful teachers and use of the best exercise equipment. I used them all, sometimes being selfish about it, and tried to keep my support group to myself.

My journey is about confidence in myself. It makes me want to tell everyone that anything is possible if you have the drive and an abundance of confidence. Be confident in yourself, but also be humble.

If you're overconfident and not humble, you'll never get the help needed. People are drawn to someone who is a leader, but a leader who is willing to listen to others. A Traumatic Brain

Injury is a game changer. And help will be needed.

Just like in life, things are going to happen: good, bad, catastrophic. They sure did for me! The real test is how you respond to adversity.

We are all going to arrive at a destination. It just a matter of how we get there. Don't be afraid of life. In fact, embrace it. You need to seize every opportunity in life by tackling and confronting adversity.

Without teamwork, the resources available to me, and the belief in myself, the name of my story wouldn't be The Golden Road. It probably would've been called The Tarnished Road.

I know life will go on and my Golden Road will continue. You'll need to somehow respond to and navigate those obstacles on your Golden Road.

##

Most photos used in this book were from private collections, others were searched and found in good faith with no copyright.